CAPE VERDEAN BLUES

PITT POETRY SERIES

Ed Ochester, Editor

CAPE VERDEAN BLUES

SHAUNA BARBOSA

UNIVERSITY OF PITTSBURGH PRESS

Published by the University of Pittsburgh Press, Pittsburgh, Pa., 15260
Manufactured in the United States of America
Printed on acid-free paper
10 9 8 7 6 5 4 3 2 1

ISBN 13: 978-0-8229-6521-3
ISBN 10: 0-8229-6521-6

Cover photograph: *Ataraxia* by Warren Keelan
Cover design by Alex Wolfe

For Robert Morales

I know you love me. You know I love you.

CONTENTS

CAPE VERDEAN BLUES

LET

my father be a pregnant palm.
Or Cesária Évora's voice
on Christmas with Sodade on her lips.
Let him be Amilcar Cabral's fist in the air.
And the pardon for all the stints
the sun fixed on his baby girl.

Let him be an instrument
in a jazz song: trombone, bass, and snare.
The ship carrying his brothers and sisters.
If rain falls on the land he can't live on,
let him be a wildflower there.

Be a dancer, be a volcano with good intentions.
Be thousands of drums shipped to Cape Verde.
The cell phones, the shirts, and the shoes inside.

Let the sky be my father on his knees.
Let the sun be my father.
When the blues melt the sun,
let me be the words he holds tight.

This week will be like the week your mother disappeared, and your now dead uncle taught you multiplayer solitaire. Bet the money you saved in high school that you will hear the chains falling. Break every chain, the gospel. Commit to thinking in terms outside of your bones. They move. Then they don't. Your insides twerk, up and down, back and forth. Gemini, this week is the accent you have, but refuse to use. It's time to move through life with your head open. Your solitude will roll down the street smoking, using language as a thing with which to shoot. Your throat will feel like a drain. Hair hugging metal. Forget about unclogging; go on with your days. Hide your face from children when crying in public. Your one good uncle will die as you dance on top a table. If you look directly into the sun, document the day anger (your mother) took your hand and did a crazy thing—held it.

SMALL TOWN & TERRIFYING

If I listen to the news tonight, I won't come.
On mute the television anchor exchange sounds
like, Do you remember what you used to do.
Looks like, Do you remember what we did to you.
I think the lady anchor's saying, I'm the only
taste you can describe without referring to notes,
my scent, the way home without roads. Man
anchor thinks she needs a new city dipped in holy
overcast, daily drama, and daily migraines
false remedied with vinegar, washcloth, cold water.
If I unmute, I could unfocus the idea of private
property. In Santo Antão, when a landowner's
animal wanders into or destroys the garden
of her neighbor, the owner of the garden seeks
punishment. I await penalty on his lap.
In Boston, everybody's plan out is to flip houses.
I'll pay for the part of my elaborate pretending,
but there's no faking, I prefer my eggs over easy
I just can't make them easy for myself.

DON'T LEAVE YOUR
SMART PHONE AT HOME

It had not occurred
to me to hit record
on vacation. I lugged
thirteen extra pounds
best explained as delirium.
Could not record,
the waves is technology,
is experience. My
experience did not occur.
Fury so gorgeous
I knelt on my sun &
carpet burned knees
in awe like the dream
where a guy is being stabbed.
In front of a crowd,
bearing witness.

EVERY YEAR TRYING TO GET MY BODY RIGHT

Frenchmen Street in your pickup truck with the broken rearview and the door I can't open from inside. What's better than New Orleans car smell, scraped toes hanging out the passenger side. I keep the window open in the event I need to summer language my mouth into prayer. A gallon of water, two crawfish sandwiches, twelve years between us. I've got that one good one: God is grace, God is good. Let us thank you for our food. A man I ate before you said, I'm sick and tired of you overfeeding yourself. For breakfast, I used to put my weight into scrubbing the stove. I stay lathered up. I stay far away from home. These languid seconds waiting for you to release me disguised as every year I've spent trying to get my body right. I'm in Brazil now, choking on humid desire, armed with another good one: What doesn't move, flies. Amen.

TAKING OVER FOR
THE '99 & THE 2000

Embraced only by fire hydrants
our preteen lives
how we knew them: the girls got boys,
the boys got money.

Peace to the faces
of boys who have now been shot dead.
Others deported to the warmer climates
of Praia, of Fogo.

Peace to the gorgeous good hair girls
now birthing boys texting boys and
phones and
de-viced or devised, we're all online thinking,

Who the fuck can throw a better looking
baby shower than me?

Uploading took over the 2000's
children of immigrants taking the best
parts of being unparented in Roxbury
and making them worst.

Quiet the dead are these days, yeah? For the watchmaking Cancers, at the end of the month, watch her get a manicure. How her four fingers caress the back of the manicurist's hand while her thumb is being shaped into a coffin. Count that embrace: count on your fingers, count in your head. Count eight clocks, they don't talk back. The clocks will keep working. Cancer keep working. Keep time. Time don't talk back. One clock says she will have your baby. Another sees you by the curtains listening to jazz in REM. The dead let light in; they use your terror. The universe wants you to stop throwing up. Three whiskeys, four hours, and later, you will find yourself over a monocle five minutes too long. For the watchmaking Cancers, at the end of the month, count eight clocks, count nine. Take a shot. With your ten fingers, tick her mouth; watch her two hands that won't hold yours. Between the 14th and 18th, lie next to her, your lesser frame a lesson. The moon is a hammock. A hammock is a moon. Loosen up, Cancer. Lie down without moving, ask how she's doing, and let the dead come.

THE GENETICS OF LEAVING

Inside, this vessel feels like the 1996 spelling bee when I forgot
u in language. Vovo left Fogo
to Praia. Now she has two sons named José.
Islands apart, I already jelly fished every memory that's stuck
inside. Saltwater
nostalgia stung, rinsed right up off me.

Vovo left and came back, not recognizing my thirteen-year-old
aunt, her new haircut
resembling the first José. I contracted. I expanded.
I pushed temporary waters behind me. I already forgot
I've got two versions of my climb. The one I swam and, I—

I only climbed this mountain to take a picture at the top,
bell-shaped bodies all forgotten.

All this bad luck because I split a pole.
If I could open my mouth
I'd ask my grandmother why
she took so long to return to her first set of fish.
I'd ask if she's aware she has two sons named the same.
She's got two versions of herself,
one in the land of a free, haircut, two, me.

As soon as you start to love a city,
a thick-bodied flight attendant touches your shoulder
walking down the aisle. Thought that was affection.

I took care of that part of myself in a complicated way.
There's only one temperature that's good enough for a mother
to bring back the u of this vessel that is no longer the you
around my neck.

MAKING SENSE OF WHAT
WE'RE MADE FOR

I like how the bottoms of my feet feel
like silence. Can you exit my whorehouse,
enter my empty? How the floor spits
gunpowder, leaving its mark on coffins.
I've a suspicion I was a little girl
dab in the middle of dancing, bestowing
rings and roses to mice in a crack house.

Sodade.

I hope you find you
before I do.

Sodade.

They've taken a beating, my feet. I know
you think pretty I'm bold, bold girls
don't die. I smile silence, shipwreck harsh
seas. My hollers vibrate a sweet magic.
I sweat violence like ceremony. Come
closer and you can hear my legs like tires
like grief in the wings of an eagle. Closer
and

Sodade.

I made myself my mother.
Then I made myself yours.

TO THE BROTHERS OF
CESÁRIA ÉVORA

I'm at the jazz bar
staring at the saxophonist
looking for the entry wound.
My curated movements
are all pretend

darkness don't equal depth.
He's looking for mind, too.
Me too is not the same
as hang in there. All rhythm
no blue like swinging

arms are all form of measurement.
The sax to body position, dead skin
cells to household dust

flying across the world
doesn't compare to noticing
your only bookmark is a pair
of scissors, to cut

means leaving the big tune.
No more pretend this place
smells how it looks outside
at dawn on September's first
fresh

turning from hopeful to who
can I talk to alive or six-feet under.
Curated sendoff,

one last wound tune
for my brothers, all colors ranging
bread, coffee, blood sausage, and
gaslight. No one wants
a black mouth brother

I know, you don't want to be
cause it's difficult to be
black, and

brown mouth with a hopeful open
no more pretend not knowing
that speaking Portuguese
at the traffic stop
won't save you.

GIRL

What you went through gon' cost you. For Sale: Body
never tampered with. For Sale: Unwanted snow blower.
Being consistently inconsistent. For Sale: Cell phone passwords.
For Sale: Not your size graduation gown never worn.
Sump pump & pipe. Those lazy expression
lovers welcomed with a yes. For Sale: Weak lovers who spit
without asking. For Sale: The ground they walk on.
A rigid plumbing tool. Flannel belonging to the photographer
met online. For Sale: The photographer's wife's website.
Fainting couch. Discontinued NYX,
wet n wild, Blast Off Burgundy lipstick by Posner.
The boat grandfather arrived on. The house grandfather died in.
For Sale: Artist condo to take photos of the flannel wearer.
For Sale: Galvanized mop bucket. How you show up
at the let out. For Sale: Gently used cloth diapers.
For Sale: Bad vibe seeds guaranteed to grow good.
For Sale: Certificate confirming Posedeia as sea-goddess.
Faint water pressure. For Sale:
Everything that broke you.

THIS WON'T MAKE SENSE IN ENGLISH

lénsu-marra n. scarf; headscarf

I've worn this wig long enough this shit is mine raise your hand
if you're too tired to wrap your real hair at night raise your
hand if you feel insecure about wrapping your hair in bed with
anyone for the first time I am laughing at my future Instagram
captions if I burn the palo santo he gifted me will it burn the
body just added to my roster

BROKE

While I study my aunt makes a few bucks with no English at the Au Bon Pain in Harvard Square. She's sweeping like it's a Saturday morning in her Cape Verdean home. Don't stop until the floor's licked clean. Make your bed like you changed your bed. Today my aunt introduces her *subrinha* to the other Cape Verdean workers, who, young and old, are mostly cleaning or organizing the croissants. I smile over, a free Americano. It takes courage or will or common sense or common courtesy or respect to dare a language not your own. When they ask me how I'm doing in broken English, I hurry toward class but today my aunt has my grandmother on her phone. *Pamódi, pamódi,* Vovo wants to know why I don't visit. She's yelling at me in Kriolu and I love how it sounds to be loved so fiercely in another language. I hear words I know and ones I don't in the voice of the only woman who braided my hair, the only woman who held my hand in her baby-soft skin. I want to ask Vovo how she's doing, but she doesn't know any English. Across the room, one woman mistakenly teaches another to say, I miss you, have a good day.

HOW'S IT GOIN' DOWN

When I moaned high,
hissed, Deeper, what I meant
was, say what you remember
of your mother giving you up.

I have gossip for you
if you have gossip for me.
When I text goodnight,
I mean tell me again

the me in this bar is
worth losing sleep over.
When I tell you I'm working
on a vision

what I mean is, bless no
triggers in this family photo.
When I say I'm at a local
jazz club in awe
like the unnamed brother
in Baldwin's "Sonny's Blues"
what I mean is,
there exists no note without
my name on it. When I tell you

to put my name on it,
you do. With a song you
can't pronounce, opaque
o, pack, unpack our scars.
We didn't last a year.

When I tell you I want to work
things out what I mean is, I knew
a man's body before my own.
Knew back pain before
I looked back and eyed my own.
The sax is killing it.

The sax is where it's going down,
it's how we hear the part, here
where it all hurts, the part when
it all hurts. I mean, the good part

of the evening. The light feels like
trick candles pleading to be relit,
the ones making themselves
wrong. Extinguished and
wandering, without a chance
for renewal.

DENIZ

This part of life should get to be longer. We crashed off a bridge in my sleep that summer you bit into an orange in order to peel it and felt embarrassed when our friends laughed out of slight disgust. You should come with a disclaimer. We learned trades with our hands but there on that bridge we were cultured on the existence of our teeth. Mine grit yours broke. Am I talking about the sun? The sun is on the list of things I make myself I tell myself. I am nothing without. Still, no. I think this is about waves. I think it started with a dream. I should come with a disclaimer. Anything you say or do may be used against you in a poem. Nature itself designed the first bridges. You're forgetting what sorrow sounds like in the dark. How to season fish. Taste the salt away on fingers. Reward yourself. Get down on your knees and eat. Forgive yourself. Another trick to being alone. I was in the air, still. Resembling how we made our first bound into a hospital room with an open window. I think it started with my mother crying while she spoke. I heard the ocean in her mouth. I think it ended with a sales associate named Deniz, meaning "sea" in Turkish.

I'M NOT DRUNK; I HAVE ONLY SWALLOWED A BONE!

In his tongue, I disappear with all the basics
to say, No, I will not marry you for documents.
Nights have never been good to me. The hour
of think this, do that. Manuel's hair curls like a ribbon
sprayed with cornstarch. He speaks to me
in Kriolu, his curls bounce with animation.

*

My mouth responds with leg locking
under a beach tent. My voice is trying to hide
in my throat; I can tell. My jaw is breaking.
About Tarrafal, the sweet stray dog
countryside where we lie, Manuel tells me how the sky
swells up like a bruise out of nowhere, like a grape
next to the sun. Language lost on every lick
placed on my back.

*

From Graciosa, Tarrafal's palm trees are
deceptively American. Detachment swells up
out of nowhere, like a bruise surprising for its size
after scratching. Tarrafal, the sea urchin
that won't sting. I need more metaphors
for hard things to swallow.

*

For fun, I let the bones of the eel get to know my mouth,
an inert place from which I only speak my native
language when fear trumps freedom. When he's driving
stick shift too fast on cobbled roads when on cobbled
roads he rears too close to stray dogs.
I work up a loose gut to say I'm not drunk;
I have only swallowed a bone!

*

Wet from Cape Verde's unremarkable humid winds,
I chip like a cheap topcoat. Permitting him a taste
of the English until I come off his tongue,
needing a name for every move it took to bring forth
the nebulous identity of rice and beans.

Learn waiting by waiting in daylight. Life used to be hair soaking feathered pillowcases on the first night. Trails of casual October sin dripping down your neck. Nights were your eyes open sinking in another fool's mouth. Scorpio, try pedaling forwards this month. Put on a song that reminds you of nothing as you wash your hair with three conditioned conditioners. Untangle indecision. Practice bantu knots and Scorpio, you've got to let them dry. Or else you can count on the texture of your hair feeling like Mercury in Retrograde. This month, life'll be a night disguised as moisturized lips, wet with pillow talk. Every time you reach for something, it'll be paper towel. Prayer won't work. If you learn waiting by waiting for the collapse of the moon, on the 18th, over brunch, water will not drip down the back of your neck. This is your time to turn yourself into one of those women who wait, forever and a day, til the bantu knots dry.

WHEN I SAY I WANT A BABY, YOU SAY YOU MISS ME THAT MUCH TOO

Let this letter find
you well as I found your well,
sullied and full, ill-timed
ocean water
on my tongue.

Summer
still feels like your head locked
in my lap. Your bareness
stepped out for a river run.

The day you discovered the sun
is a noun you can't touch,
I licked the mole on your cheek
excited to make amends
with a verb I can't love.

I watched you in winter
unfold like a travelling tragedy;
drunk, womb, memory,
sunk, uncertainty.

A body's not just a body.

What is surveillance if not
a world where you are the man?

You survey yet you don't learn.

I howl your name, a woman
raised by wolves, inept were we.
A soft fog dims
all lights and chokes me. Please.

THIS WON'T MAKE SENSE IN ENGLISH

*gudjadu adj. sprouted; bud; el éra nóba inda, ku se mama ~,
she was still a virgin with her breasts sprouting*

Living single tongue not sweet enough yet still mourning Queen
Latifah with the key around her neck

SELF-PROCLAIMED SAD BOY

Everyone I want to write to is dead.
So I meet sad boy on the busy Internet streets,
traffic covered in drunk people. Perhaps I can explain
how they always come back to the house,
like loose lies and friendly fires
making vintage every Gchat.

He was New York new.
Crept up on me right before the beat dropped,
immediately after I realized
I conveniently live in a great place
for a mental breakdown.
We meet in Boston where I hide my face
behind silent smoked sheets we fold together.
I'm clenching the end.

Sad boy quit me seven times
after the smell of my whiskey damp tongue
made a tattoo on his back.
I want less from me and more for me.
So I write another tiny letter,
the matters of men who are not mine
do not matter to me.

I say sad boy being admired
must be lonely IRL. In three bridges time,
we drank our dinner, listened to Janet Jackson,
Do you want this? Can you handle this?
Do you want the war that comes
with this skin? Well, come here then.

RE THE DENTIST AND HIS NEW FAMILY

Teeth person will not eat beef unless the mother cooks it.

The I would like to say: Fuck your baby.

Mother will cook beef if son buys it.

A teeth person walks about the quad on what a person is suspected to walk upon.

A person of teeth. Teeth own a person.

I am doing well. I am having a baby.

Some sets of teeth walk. Teeth person,

I have had dreams about your baby. Teeth on carefully.

I was once a baby, now, damaged goods, now, a dent in the corner of a $1,500 laptop, precious technology.

Communicate a stain that would be refused by the local favorite dry cleaner.

Teeth person taught me ruin.

Exit without having entered.

List what's known about teeth person other than teeth person
will not eat beef unless mother cooks it.

Teeth person once walked upon, on, with tongue to say: I want
an artist.

The mirthful artist wonders,

Did teeth person ever declare: I want a bank teller?

Teeth, bank teller, baby.

Show the I those teeth. Show the I that money.

WELCOME BACK

after Etheridge Knight

Welcome back, Ms. B: Love of My Life—
How's your identity problem?—your culture
problem? you / are / pickling
your lesson—
Gotta / watch / out
for the "Ol' Lesson": Love of My Life.
How's your acid
problem?—your weed, Adderall, Lexapro
and Lithium too?—your lustful problem—
How's your weight problem—your eating
problem? How's your lying and cheating
and staying out all / night long?

Welcome back, Ms. B: Love of My Life.
How's your money / saved up / don't know
what to do with it problem? You quit—
Your job problem. How's your small breast
problem?—your might buy some
titties problem? How's your Plan B?
Welcome back, Ms. B: Love of My Life
How's your used to / write / that boy
in jail / until he got shot & killed problem?
How's your stalker problem?—
Your fucking too many in the crew?

You don't feel magic / ain't never loved no one
problem? How's your book
problem? / Ain't been published /
haven't read your lover's book problem?
How's your might go to Dominican Republic
to fix your waist / what you sit on / put
your / breasts in her & his mouth problem?
The porn problem?
Never let go / don't love / don't leave
please need me problem? Your want to fuck
everywhere but a bed / in the dark / problem?
And your crushing pills / crushing dignity
out of pity problem?
How's your drinking?—your thinking?

You still paranoid? Still bipolar?
Still scared shitless? Still wanna die?
Welcome back, Ms. B: Love of My Life.
How's your language problem? Understand
and won't speak to save your
grandmother's heart problem?
How's your / everything is about pussy
and race problem?—Your enough problem—
You gotta watch out for the "Ol' Lesson."

How's your social network?
Your / why / did / he / just / post
a / photo / of / his / girlfriend / knowing
I / would / see / it?
Your unfollowing triggers?
How's your checking the last time / who
he's following / Why hasn't he responded
to your hateful, don't mean it text messages
problem? Your want to be a rapper problem?—
Your back on the bed, against the wall
on the pavement—just let it come / problem?
Welcome back, Ms. B: Love of My Life.
You gotta watch out for the "Ol' Lesson."

When he speaks of how wet Cape Verdean women get, tell him that's the rain that never hits the land. The rain that never hits the land is despair. The rain that never hits the land is refuge. The rain that never hits the land is the sea anticipating cautious pregnant plants, planning the spark of an open mouth. Spend his birthday in Paris. Do not wish him well. Sweat and cigarette smoke and blisters tearing down your dancing body on the night of his day. Unaware unsettled, put un before it all. Before the weight of those black drums on a moving ship to Cape Verde, all those American 'goods' in search of recovery.

FOREIGN SUMMER REMEMBERED IN TRAFFIC

The goats inside the shed remember my shirt
lifeless collapsed on the side of the pool.
Here I am shedding empty casings
on the hour before dawn.
Other than the accent you place on my name
I don't understand a word from you.
There is no old hat. There is no one I miss.
What am I going to give
the children I won't have?
If I could get rid of anything, it'd be traffic.
I am open for you.
I am open to deceit, at the Basilica
you ask if skin and bone
are just the shaping of trees.
Sitting in traffic experiencing
a lightshow of sun hitting
leafless branches, hitting me
as the bus goes down the highway.
Here I am remembering the shed
outside the pool where I learned
in Kriolu, the word for condom
is the same as a baby's shirt.

Forcing forget on a Saturday in September is how you arrive at the sea. To address the time of day would mean to reveal how time spends itself around. Sand dollars have no heart. Ask the doctor to get it in writing and faxed to the nearest machine: Sand Dollars Have No Heart. Are people the skeletons of the lives they create? Is your location determined by physical capability or you are where you are from the wash up? Aries, here is what you need to know: organisms of the sea cannot be repulsed by chipped toenail polish. Put your feet in. Walk in shallow oceans with suede sandals. Make skeleton picking your brave new hobby like gathering what's left of things fallen while you bathe. In bed with yourself, terror shall leave no part unkissed.

TONE'S POSTURE

It's true—he will not call
no matter how close you place the phone to your breasts.
He carries a large briefcase filled with affliction.
If you don't duck you'll never learn that the wind is not failure.
Be quick &
you will still have time for dawn's festivities.
When your phone is on the floor he will flood, you
will hear the melancholy in the back of his throat.
You know better than to accompany the act, every time
you think you spot him pulling up to the train station,
bend down slowly, tie the wind's shoes.
He'll miss your head when he actually comes,
flaunting all that restrained equilibrium.

FLUSH PAST THE FERRY

Two brief girls or two turkey vultures came lurking
on the bike route outside the church.
A wedding is just a speck in Edgartown.
To confess love while it's under your nails
is to confess I've been drinking tap water.
It comes highly recommended.
Two brief girls or two turkey vultures
chase plastic into the ocean.
High tide and destiny continue on.
Don't feel bad, the rest of the world still works.

Onions wouldn't cut for you if you asked nicely. The way deer won't voluntarily bleed on your lap. Imagine a deer hits you while en route to mass-produced cheesecake. Days do not ruin themselves, but whose day is ruined here? Mid-week, in the middle of primetime, the cable company cuts the wrong wire. Why isn't that writer you're fucking writing about you? Fancy yourself the small of his back. Squat the small of his island as you well up wet with every text message. No two arrive alike. Take the day's juiced morning, blinds wide open and touch yourself toward his window (he finds this beautiful and pointless, but more beautiful). Reckon the ways you are never and always wrong. Now you're both outside awaiting the technician, listening to each other miss visuals you're too lazy to create.

SOMETHING AFRICAN WITH A K

In Virginia, years after, you got into gardening. Because you had lost your hair, you wanted to watch things grow. The baby you almost had would have set the table. You like to think of a girl because Tony said on the trolley back to his house that he would want to name her after his mother. But you thought her name was ugly. Despite your father being African, you thought the name was *too* African. But you love its American meaning. You never once cooked for Tony in the dingy apartment overlooking the Boston skyline he shared with his brother. You think the baby would have been this tall girl who set the table, a girl named after her grandmother. Koshi. Kochi. Koshie. A silent letter anywhere, but you don't remember because you said no. You told me you would call her Grace.

GREAT GENERAL OF
IMPOSSIBLE BATTLES

The day I buried Bob
you went bowling
with a med student
I used to advise
on thrift store fashion.
Called you 19 times
wondered if she wore
the overalls or clownish
shapeless dress
I told her, is, absolutely
in this time
of year when you are
feeling like it's time
to walk around inside
of your own freak
show.

Bob used to phone me
dressed in worry. He'd
heard I'd carried
my mattress outside
and slept in the dirt
so you'd know
I was ready
for battle.

You were not even home.

On the phone for hours
without mention of you
I asked Bob how to know
a good poem. He said,
Where did the poet
study writing?
Where did the poet
study fucking?

You brought me
to the thrift store
after I first stayed
the night.
My clothes stained
with confusion
damp even,
while I picked out
a plaid polo shirt
with silver buttons
running everywhere.

After I viewed the new
Bob just lying there,
I called you
from my home phone.
I still have a home phone.
You answered
on ring 20 but
I needed more ringing.

SOMEWHERE THERE'S A BABY ON THE LINE

Somewhere there's a baby on the line. I want to be careful with what comes next. Your face still a strange place I visit when I need an alley to watch my back in. A baby on the line. Not a kitchen restaurant line getting dressed fermented rhubarb sitting quietly. The kind of line two people create when only one wants to stay. In the park where I loved you publicly now stands a little man pounding two drums led by an elder. For dinner, I'll kiss the baby's body before freezing. Dead as in not here yet. Dead as in not my baby. This is not a lesson in frozen dinners. It's asking myself to stop investigating your personal life. Drums were certainly made for you. They make all that noise. They don't ask questions.

THIS WON'T MAKE SENSE IN ENGLISH

pasada [pasu] n. step; ~ di ómi, grasa-l mudjer, short visit;
badja ~, dance the pasada dance

Your freckles wholesome your steps leading me I am sucking my
stomach in as much as I can this dance leading me into nights
full of you full in you full off you fueled up can you pull my
dress down for me can you feel this dance leading us to the
end of the night I already need a ride home already nostalgic
about the crooked space between your teeth countless points
of contact we're holding each other like this short visit is the
definition of consumption

Fireworks start in June. You will take them for gunshots if you haven't heard a pistol go off uncomfortably close to your head. If you haven't heard a group of boys ride by your house and there! Three bullets. First last and security. Leo, shower before your roommates. Hot water rare as someone when you need them most. A grateful heart shall not despair. On the 14th day of this month, the door will weep behind you. You are more than the walls men rap about. Greater than the walls that managed not to collapse in high school, walls that got higher in college. Walls, easy enough, keep men in a job line. Welfare line. Funeral line. Touching the weep, the ceiling will play the trombone. The floor beneath you will dance.

BIG SUN COMING STRONG THROUGH THE MOTEL BLINDS

Before you closed the blinds
on our first morning together
you left me naked under a Haitian
quilt. This was not the time I waited
for you in a black tulle dress
and nothing else. Tulle against
my ass against my thighs
against everything I thought I was.
This is what a wife would do,
you note. By this time,
you had already touched me well.
You're a different kind of professional.
There are technical terms for what
I'm doing except I left my big words
at home. Except I wanted light
to come through the blinds.
What makes this complicated
to detail is how special my body
felt to be chosen by you.
What a fading place of grace
for false exploration. Is it truly
an honor to please a man who
doesn't know that being stalked
means the number of hotel cookies
I ate while waiting for him is on record.

What an honor to please a man
who doesn't know,
that wanting to mourn secretly,
is the same as doing it.

GPS

says there's a Duane Reade a mile from Chinatown. It's 96 degrees on a Saturday. My legs are wet. Sweat stings my contact lenses. I'm coming for you. The taxi driver is West African. You are my sister, he says. I'm changing my bra, my shirt, in the backseat, while he keeps his eyes on the Lincoln Tunnel and his thoughts on women who are slaves to their men. I stare at his name and badge number and wonder what his wife in Africa looks like. I wanted to ask what his American woman looks like. A lot of time passes and I think about my old West African lover and feel bad for being so American. Be more like your father's side; he's so involved we get lost. I get to you. My hair the size of my hips. I awkwardly tell you I like your t-shirt. You say It's just a grey t-shirt. You kiss the back of my legs and I want to cry. Only the sun has come this close, only the sun.

THIS WON'T MAKE SENSE IN ENGLISH

banhâ v. take a bath; surround
banhera n. bathtub; tub
banhóka n. sweet bath
banhu n. bath; swim; tuma ~, take a bath, take a shower
banu n. wave; oscillation

What a waste of energy riding an elevator alone one more person'll make it worth it sinking comes in two the howling then the tombstones buried in snow the only little marker from home if you've got bad energy take a dip at the beach sea salt'll bring you right back to the time you were so happy you inboxed your tub sudded body for a Hollywood star

Be a bird this month. Be built in speakers. When you find your honey eclipsed behind licorice lips, wisdom body yourself into a feverish chant. Remember when you used to be so mad at Biggie for killing Tupac. Turn that storyless scar into a symphony. He's so new; you love when he calls you names. When you don't know how he could live outside of you. When rich black ain't less black. Be the exotic accent, over the e, fuck like one of those neon signs that flinch. Shoulders make ceilings tangible. Be alluring when you break. You are a furnished room. You mourn persons unknown. You belt out dear mamas wrapped in rap. You are more than body goals. Your wisdom body is mounted at the tips of praying hands. Your wisdom body will trump the trauma. Be a bird this month. Be turned on by your own energy. The only cure for this hangover is you.

THERE'S SOMETHING SO DEEPLY GRATIFYING ABOUT WELCOMING YOUR MOTHER INTO YOUR HOME AND OFFERING HER A MEAL AS NOURISHMENT AND THANKS

When small introduces itself as a dirty word
I contemplate how to put food down.
Each early morning at 4:17 a.m.

an operating system restores
its warless ocean of information.
Within hours following deletion

I wake with less interest
than having slept with. I forget
the flavor of your peroxide mouth after

hours of Facetime. Your beard
requires a search engine
of its own. I search for me too.

Using altered keystrokes like am I
really the baby my mother carried drunk?
Am I the operating system? Am I hungry?

While at dinner being fucked
crawled into my mind. Hula-hooping
wine glasses. My mom needs to know

that it's okay to take your socks off
at the beach. The idea of feeling a delight
not associated with fried shellfish is

a thing to feel. But now
I'm thinking about our weight.
There are no women with our bodies on TV.

AND I KNOW THAT SHE FEELS BEAUTIFUL —DO WE HAVE CANCER

We talked at length about her cervix and her decision to no longer perm her hair. A woman at the Cape Verdean salon in Roxbury told her, You are more beautiful with long black hair. I told her they're bitches, even though they're my people. I stared at her curly Sierra Leone sunset. She said when she takes a bath she can feel where they've cut. We have a lot in common, although I have not felt my own. Fingers move my unsettled hair around to hide the bald spots. She said we look alike when we met for lunch today. The pain is back and I feel underdressed. A wave of bare elbows digging trenches in the tabletops.

Wake up, let the Internet comfort you in its lazy web. Ask Mother Google about wildfires. She will moan, The fire will pass before your house burns down. No one's thinking about you. The ringing in your ear is sirens. Begin your departure by brushing yourself against the shower wall until you; you start to fall from the clinging. Repeat. Like rituals to make you beautiful (lemon water in the morning). Rituals to make you pleasant (therapy). Say you stay, know that you still have time to build yourself of what the rich want. Chase the rule of the road, the rules of your house. Be the boat in the water, the bridge lifting its arms making way for the things you carry. You can even be a car this month, Aquarius. Speed across frantic flames; let the Internet break itself in your rich wet presence.

31-YEAR-OLD LOVER

Draped in a Malibu mansion
dressed in my aunt's blonde wig
and her long, black suede coat,

I wanted to be Lil' Kim.

If I had to name myself, my name
would be on every corner, meaning the promise
of plenty, like the abundance of stores
selling blonde Barbies and boy toy
soldiers who could use a break.

The moment news from afar approaches the rim
of my callous glass of Cab, my name
would already be your fragile song

crushed under the weight of encounter,
as you found me crushed under the weight of a car.

Drunk on provocative statements, I was still alive
when I reached for you, how you turned away,
how you glazed past me, demanding I let go.

Only some know when it's time to chill.

If I had to name myself, it would be hardcore.
Kim's legs wide open. Hardcore

like how you won't learn to drive
a car that'd play Gil Scott-Heron
for you. Hardcore

like how I've hardly been
sleeping without you.

SIMONE

with her big knees ballerina skirt. Imagined her in this church the ink on the back of her hands fading falling down her raised arms her mouth slightly whispering to her most high. How we'd look in a photograph. How I'd look to myself to our friends loved ones smiling how we'd look together. Wide knees and thighs glasses dolling tints of blue her hair taking comfort around one shoulder. The end of class brings Simone close to me. A man I don't know lifts her attention I walk away hungry then stop rustle in my bag watch them talk. Each day feels like a phone call a sound with good news a promise to return with more information. Imagined making love to her not knowing where to begin.

YOUR EYES BLINK FIVE-MINUTE MILES

Knot by knot I pulled my hair
out on the ferry. Who knows what
these arms are doing above my head.
I would lick my own face
to taste the sea. I would take
your bulbs for their brightness. People
who enjoy life make me uncomfortable.
How could you love the quarry so but sleep
gripping your own button down shirt
for freedom? My hair was playing
the thorn to your eyes as our ears
our ears mistook wind in the trees for the ocean.

It's profoundly normal to become fragile while ordering coffee. The barista wants your money. The barista wants your name. Say his, while pretending to look for change. Against your tongue is the only direction he goes. Say his name, and then say yours. This week, imagine trying to have a body and a break. Open legs come easy, but that's not grief. Grief is the patch of hair you find on your thighs as you walk out of the coffee shop and head toward the disco in high waisted shorts. The key to monogamy is dancing. Allow his name to teach you what you taught him. On the blackest night, tame the madness by losing your face inside another woman. What you long for and desire inside of your home has everything and nothing to do with what goes on outside. When you get back to the party, make sure you know what you're partying for.

YOU WILL, INDEED, ALWAYS BE
THE SAME PERSON AFTER VACATION

Mexican tacos in Paris
look like thick rolled cigars,
if cigars had meat inside.
They dance Bachata.
Their feet move in confusion.

The sirens here remind me
of a wretchedness
I cannot place,
maybe something I heard
in a book. European unrest

over deboned white fish.
In Le Marais, I told a Canadian
from Morocco, *here lies a chef.*
I felt his fingers tremble
as he felt my palms for shucking oysters.

Nothing in its right place
but there we were
walking in the time of Daguerre
on water with our hands
on the mouths of our purses.

Go to Paris. Let it change you.
When you arrive back
warily on a buddy pass,
you say you are not easily impressed.
In the Seine of truth, you are easily
lonely
at the Eiffel,

in the Louvre, you smile
with a nose your father called big.
Into the camera you go,
your thrown self
in front of Mona Lisa.

AFTER FINDING A HAIR IN MY FOOD AT ROXBURY'S FIRST GENTRIFIED CAFÉ

I didn't want my money back.
Of course I want my money
back. I tell my kids, Ask for
what you want. Speak up.
Use your words. Want. There's
a strand of hair in my food
and my hair ain't that straight.
That's what I said. I said
let's try again. I want fingers
in my mouth. I love the worst
city beach. My body been
made like steel, black like
the gun I found in my cousin's
Timberland bag. I was terrified
to touch. If I knew what I
know, that I'd be showing up
to the party smelling like
yellow rice and bacalhau,
like yesterday's coffee, I
would have touched it, his gun.
Having your life together is
the shell casing in this poem.

Don't think: Your body will
ever be yours. Though last
night I touched myself, green
garlic on my tongue, spiced
Goya in my veins.

When the rain stops, go to the top of the royal fortress not far from the two towering churches to see the scenery and smell the damp of the earth your knees will dig into later tonight. Go to her house. Experience her at breakfast. Your blouse and hair will get caught in the rain that turns the yard, all of the city green. Chat with her father about corn crops. Tell him you are the woman he's expecting to show up with fertilizer for all the farmers growing produce typically not found in the old city. When you arrive, ask her to take you over the base of it. Go to steal the fennel head, to see her barefoot, to gather enough of her to do business with.

BLOSSOM

The deal with being struck by lightning is there are no deals
for the lonely hearted.

No deal when I said I love you too to my lover of three weeks.

I miss my cat, even he doesn't belong to me.

On the Vineyard women appear in the living rooms of white
fenced homes.

They all look the same. They all shout come inside me

to the only room on the bottom floor.

My lover would be jealous if he knew the way I touched
women.

All shoulders taste of potential. All lashes close doors for me.

I know losing involves lying

on the ground trying to lift myself up. Had I accepted the
bottom floor

lightning could not have flowed through this silent carpel as a blossom.

Flowers travel only when I carry them. I am the most attractive flower

when I'm standing alone next to everything.

NOT CRAZY JUST AFRAID TO ASK

if she had a baby born with an addiction.
Need I've learned, is one of those months
when I am not lonely it's just that April
is the cruelest month.
I'm not lonely

it's the wind blowing back grateful
blowing forth complacent. Fortune says
I'm not crazy

just one of those people who can walk
in the house walk right by the dog.
Learned a long time ago that swearing
on God when lying
won't kill my mother won't kill
the neighborhood boys. Nothing
special about this year is the truth.
But the sun

is out today cars are being cared for
in a novelty phase sort of way.
The dogs 'round here walk their men
up and down the dead grass still
blooming in the year
I must be wrong about.

The second week of the first month with her name strepped on your throat, meet her at your favorite store. Just don't meet her halfway. You will need a map but no directions. Libra, you will never meet her. This week, get to know her acumen. Shout the answers without her asking. She will never ask. Be innocent until the day comes. Let spiders live, let your fears jaywalk across your chest. This week, today, your ears will get hot at the cut of her teeth when you tell her you already have someone. Pretend where you'll first meet is not a waste of a great city. The city you will ask to pick her up in. She will ask you, Where? & you will type, In the air. The second week of the first month with her name strepped on your throat, study every comment on every photo. Pretend she is not a waste of a great city. Though she makes you feel like a God, do not forget she is not the one to leave home for. She is a practice. Smile while her tongue hangs above you like a wind chime. Blow. Blow. Bow. Libra, she is a ritual. You're trembling. Fall asleep like you mean it. Like it's late night after the raspberry pie your girlfriend will make in your mom's house. Fall asleep like you mean it—go to sleep with her profile open.

HOW TO END THINGS WELL

So what if someone finds you in a bathroom
kissing an archaeologist like you've just met.
Minimize his body into your body of work.
Hop off. Mid-ride.

Make a list of other things you can choke on:
candle wax, eucalyptus, string lights.
Eat so much you start to become the thing:
candle wax, eucalyptus, string lights.

Make a list of things you wouldn't buy.
Clothespins. Drape yourself over yourself over
the archaeologist who's a rapper who asked
if you carry lotion in your purse.

AN EMAIL RECOVERED FROM TRASH

Oct. 5, 2:14 p.m. Re: Home Swap

Somewhere a woman's lease is up. Two numbers on speed dial: Boston's best hospital for bullets and a real estate agent who aced his license exam, gels his hair. The firm is neutral for us to discuss. The woman calls him looking for a four-bedroom apartment. To keep from laughing before the joke hits, he quietly gags on his breath as he says, I know just from her name that she has Section 8. His candle quartz skin burns pink with delight. We are never together for too long.

He's nothing like you. Not brown, not a creative. This story to say: I pray for you on the toilet every morning. I ask that you are lurking on my Instagram daily. A hole in my heart for the nights I made PowerPoint presentations of your body. My little discoveries. You take your shirt off now. Mostly, I ask that you thank me now and then and that you remember your face is a home.

Hey, don't make this about race.

I know black men who gel their hair because it's what keeps them together. This bit to say, I'm not sure I know how to fuck someone who is not afraid for his life.

Am I a millennial or am I dead.

I pray you're creating. Someone different. Can you tell from my name, I'm still in search of a place to stay? I'm creating too, an aching homemade exit with reaction holes.

SELF ON THE FIRST DATE

You need the sun if you want to stop
fast action. The sun wins every single time.
The way it stands above you like everything
is going as planned, as thought. How it shines
on pregnant women on broken bikes
and bones, on unplanned pregnancies.
I'm sweating underneath the same purple pleated skirt
I got hit by a car in, or collided with a car in
or the sun opened its mouth
blew me to the ground in.
It looks different tonight.
Some kind of photo grid meant to be read
from right to left,

and I keep telling the story of being hit by a car
because I can't remember
if the driver had his blinker on. I couldn't stop
then I fell on my left side. In the street
so close to where I work,
a pregnant woman stops to ask if I'm okay.
The shape of her stomach from the concrete.
A coffee mug.

This is what comes to me in a dream: a huge belly
by an old dentist husband who is expecting
with his new lover. Going to appointments alone
walking around the office without a ring on.

There has to be a poem in looking this good
then dying on a bike. No helmet but a purple
pleated skirt. Sometimes at the light, my thick
thighs wear my shorts and men beep.

Photography is not about moments.
The rule of thirds makes a perfect sunset.
The worst time to take a photo is in the
middle of the day. I don't carry mace.

The first thing you touch at the bar is my hair.
What you unearth you name volume. You
are named after a saint who carried a sword.

The second thing you touch is my lips.

I want to take a photo of you. All directives come
together. Fill the frame let the subject dominate
the image. Get as close as you possibly can.

The third thing you touch is a complex area
named by Natacha in high school. Chichos.

You reference conflicts in the Middle East.
There's no time for spot metering. Your eyes
are moving too fast, you're casting all the light
even when you describe me as full of hope, labeling
everything as up and coming as on the rise
as getting there. I'm ignorant to international
conflict. I started in the womb with my own.
Mostly unaware but I know disturbance. Bullet wounds
in Beirut. Bullet wounds in Boston. Your sword
is in the way you stare with openness.
Men don't share where I'm from.

I feel your knuckles as if I know how a surgeon's knuckles
should knead. I think they're soft.
You show me every spot where they are not. I want
to lick the redness until I see a boy on the train ride home
staring out the window. His father wants to know
if there's anything good out there. Horrible
he whispers, but he doesn't turn his curly head.

THIS WON'T MAKE SENSE IN ENGLISH

kanala v. travel; walk; get out of the house

I told my uncle I forgive him then I walked to the dance floor

LIBERATION

I count gulls until they spasm
into numbers, until I grasp
a number never uttered. I ration
dignity like crackers to last

when my own words pan
dust into the mouth of a little gull.
I am a cracker to the plan.
Little gulls are black and full.

Little girls are running around
in pink two pieces. I call for cover,
an unspecific temp job, brown
as the wanting of erasure.

On the last day of work,
my boss said being black
is a box for checking. I smirked
and danced my hips inside the square.

Little gulls feed me not.
I like beaches, and I like counting
until I reach a number rot-
ten with plans. I'm just lounging

on a beach chair waiting
for the girls' laughter as the gulls hang
like check marks. Boxing black slang.
My noise so liberating
it asks to be no one.

ACKNOWLEDGMENTS

My warmest gratitude to the journals and editors for publishing versions of this work:

A Bad Penny Review, Atlas Review, Awl, Boston Mayor's Office of Arts and Culture, *Colorado Review, Mass Poetry, Minnesota Review, No Tokens Journal,* PANK, *Rhino, some mark made, Sundog Lit, Virginia Quarterly Review.*

One time for the readers of letsjusteatcheese.

To my parents, Roberta Taylor, Luisa Barbosa, Irlando Barbosa, thank you for carrying me, feeding me, for giving me this warm, strange light.

To my siblings India Taylor, Kyla Barbosa, Aina Lott, Malick Barros, Nisaiah Barbosa—thank you for the constant reminder that everything I do is to and for y'all.

Thamani Tomlin Norton, thank you for allowing me to sit on top of your washing machine.

Bob Morales, I am working out my issues. By my 200th birthday, I will be perfect. I will also probably be in a jar.

Adriana Cloud, Michalla DaSilva, Nakita Barros, Joey and Zane Barbosa, Caron Taylor, Damon Coleman, Denise DePina Dubuisson, Waverly Coleman, Amanda Barros, Courtney Villón, Tania DeBarros, Leah Veaudry, Telma Tavares, Jenny Tavares, Nicole Vengrove Soffer, Sydney Brown, Sue Rainsford, and Laura Gill; thank you for your tremendous love, encouragement, and support, thank you for the listening, reading, dancing, eating, wine, whiskey, words, memes, prayers, cards, crystals, candles, sage, patience—thank you for watering my plants. Thank you for showing me what it means to feel at home in the world.

Special delivery kind of thanks to Joshua Bell, thank you for 9:17. Deepest appreciation to the faculty and students at the Bennington College MFA program. Thank you to Megan Mayhew-Bergman, Kathleen Graber, Ed Ochester, Gregory Pardlo, Major Jackson, Mark Wunderlich. My Rockport loves: Simeon Berry, Abigail Mumford, Heather Hughes, thank you. For the time and space to write, thank you to the Martha's Vineyard Writing Residency and the Writers' Room of Boston.

To everyone who's ever said keep going,

keep going.